Emotional Facelift

Understanding Liberation from Negative Emotions Without Doing Time in a Monastery!

Dennis E. Bradford, Ph.D.

Publisher's Notes

ISBN 978-1-940487-17-5

Acknowledgements

I thank all those who helped me, directly or indirectly, to write this book. The truth is that it took a lifetime to write it and it would be impossible to name everyone individually who contributed.

Of course, I alone am responsible for any and all intellectual, grammatical, or typographical errors.

Related Books by the Same Author

Introduction to Living Well

Are You Living Without Purpose?

Mastery in 7 Steps

How to Survive College Emotionally

Personal Transformation

The Meditative Approach to Philosophy

Love and Respect

Getting Things Done

It's Not Just About the Money!

Table of Contents

Preface to the Reader

If you are an experienced fisherman, you have learned that fish like structure. Instead of preferring to be exposed to predatory larger fish, they prefer to be in or near underwater structures such as weed beds, drop-offs, logs, or human artifacts such as sunken boats or ships or at least to be in schools of related fish. Isolated fish are simply in more peril.

Our minds are like fish in the sense they prefer thoughts that are related to or thoroughly embedded in other thoughts. The phrase 'emotional well-being' is complicated in the sense that it involves not only two concepts (namely, the concept of an emotion and the concept of well-being) but lots of other thoughts to which it is related. After all, the way that we understand something is never as an isolated object but rather by noticing its similarities and differences to other things.

My purpose is to encourage you to detach from any beliefs about emotions that are obstructing your emotional well-being (your living well emotionally, your flourishing emotionally, your freedom from unwanted emotions). Yes, it's only theory, but it's important theory. Why? Once your thoughts about emotions are aligned with reality you'll be able to begin to practice emotional well-being. Once you begin practicing properly, the quality of your emotional life will quickly improve. As long as you keep practicing properly, those improvements will not only last but increase until death.

Until you question the beliefs about emotions that you already have and eliminate the obstructive ones, you'll simply stay stuck emotionally. Your emotional life will *never* significantly improve. It's false that emotional well-being happens accidentally. Therefore, if you want your emotional life to improve significantly, then you've no choice but to examine your beliefs about emotions, discard those you find wanting, and replace them with better ones.

Once you regularly begin thinking better about emotions, with some practice you'll quickly begin feeling better emotionally. For example, if you are suffering acutely right now from grief, anger, fear, loneliness, or any other unwanted emotion or cluster of negative emotions, you may **hope** again that you need not stay stuck, that emotional well-being really is a genuine option for you.

The reason that's the case is because there's a very important difference between thinking about emotional well-being and, say, thinking about physical well-being.

Suppose that you have a whole body that is neither injured nor diseased. Suppose, too, that you are overweight and that you want to free yourself from that condition. So you go to your personal physician for an examination and a plan of action that includes eating well and exercising well. As long as you believe that your physician is an expert, you do not have to have a sophisticated understanding of physiology to carry out that plan. That's good – otherwise, you would also have to go to medical school or at least do a lot of reading and studying to become an expert yourself before being able to lose a significant percentage of body fat in a lasting way. Fortunately for you, it's possible to lose it by following an expert's advice even if you do not understand why the expert gave you that advice.

The reason for that is because your *thoughts don't determine your percentage of body fat.* Instead, it's your genetics and environment (including your eating and exercise habits) that determine your percentage of body fat.

The reason for the dissimilarity between emotional well-being and physical well-being is that your **thoughts do determine your emotions.** As I argue in what follows, emotions essentially are thoughts. So improving how you think about them can have a speedy positive effect upon your degree of emotional well-being. How?

Directly attacking a powerful unwanted emotion fails. If you have ever directly tried to dissolve your grief at the death of a loved one, how well did that go?

However, indirectly attacking one can work quickly and thoroughly. The reason is because emotions are consequences of causal sequences. A critical belief is always a part of such sequences. Changing or eliminating that belief can yield a better outcome.

It's wise to be skeptical about this. In fact, it's wise to be skeptical of all my claims; you'd be a fool not to doubt them. Please treat all my statements as if they were questions. After all, others have misled you before, haven't they?

If the evidence I marshal in favor of my claims is as strong as I believe it is, then your skepticism will quickly fade.

On the other hand, it's important not to be negative. For example, if you are attached to the belief that nobody flourishes emotionally, all you are doing is guaranteeing that you will never flourish emotionally and never enjoy any significant emotional improvement. Those who are stuck being fools are stuck being fools.

In other words, you must be open to improving your understanding to benefit from reading this. If you are close-minded, I cannot help you live better emotionally. Why? Nobody is able to help you live better emotionally. Furthermore, you aren't even able to help yourself.

So, if you are serious about living better emotionally, please detach from whatever beliefs you have right now about emotions. Just set them aside for now. Open your mind by challenging them. If you accept the ideas presented here, then you can discard those old ones permanently and replace them with better ones. If you do not accept the ideas presented here, then you can always go back to your old ideas.

Please examine your own beliefs. At least when it comes to emotional flourishing, please question how you think about emotions.

The only way to live well is to live an examined life. The reason for that is that living well (living wisely, mastering life) never happens accidentally or magically. It's always the result of a deliberate process. Living well is difficult; it's not easy. If we want to live well, we need to examine the alternatives to select the most suitable one.

Here's a good way to think about this. The world is in incessant flux. If you don't keep examining your beliefs to keep them updated, they'll become more and more obsolete. Acting on the basis of obsolete beliefs makes life unnecessarily difficult. So regularly examining beliefs can make living better easier. After all, old beliefs don't delete themselves.

Except for laziness, there's no reason not to live an examined life. If examination reveals a better way to live, then you'll obviously have benefitted from your examination. If it doesn't, you'll still have benefitted from your examination because at least you'll understand better why certain options are poorer than what you are now doing, which boosts confidence, and you won't need to change what you are already doing.

There are two kinds of methods for emotional flourishing, the proactive and the reactive. Although I recommend both, I only consider <u>the reactive method</u> in what follows.[1] Let's suppose that you are reading this because you are in the grip of some powerful negative emotion and want to free yourself. (There are other good reasons for reading it. For example, even if you feel fine now, you realize that good fortune may not always smile upon you and life will sooner or later hit you with situations, related either to yourself or to loved ones, such as aging, illness, and death that may leave you suffering from a powerful negative emotion or even from more than one simultaneously.) If so, realize that your ability to concentrate is diminished by your current emotional condition. So be very patient with yourself as you gradually absorb the ideas presented here; it simply may take you longer than normal to understand them. I encourage you to read this book slowly at least twice.

An inability to concentrate is a common trait of powerful emotions: when we are seized by one, our range of focus narrows. The more powerful the emotion, the more our range of focus typically narrows in the sense that it becomes more and more difficult to think about anything else.

It feels really good to be able to focus single-mindedly on whatever we choose. Someone who lives well emotionally always has that ability. When we become absorbed in some task, we perform it better than we otherwise would. Furthermore, time- consciousness and self-consciousness temporarily vanish as we actually become what we are doing. That kind of focus is characteristic of mastery.

Unfortunately, you were not educated as a child about emotional well-being, emotional mastery. Nobody explained to you either how to reduce the frequency with which you are afflicted by unwanted emotions or how to get rid of them when you suffer from them. The result is predictable: **few people flourish emotionally**. As you are probably aware, lots of adults look good and smell good, but typically their thoughts and emotional lives are chaotic and unsatisfying.

Learning how to flourish emotionally is part of learning how to master life. Mastery requires full attention. Acts performed with only partial attention bring little reward. If you decide that something is worth doing, do it while paying full attention. The Buddha: "If anything is worth doing, do it with all your heart."[2]

You have the ability to **master life**. Yes, it's **difficult**. It takes the right kind of practice over an extended period of time. On the other hand, it's so **simple** that any normal human being can do it. It doesn't even require literacy. [I have attempted to explain clearly why that's the case in other books such as Introduction to Living Well.]

You are a normal human being. That's true even if you happen to be suffering acutely right now. So, please don't despair.

There are two tasks that confront you. First, assuming that you are hurting emotionally, get back to normal emotionally. What you learn here will help you to do that. There's no good reason not to transform acute emotional distress into emotional normalcy. If it's available to you, consider getting some help from a psychiatrist or clinical psychologist to resume normalcy. Second, once you are normal again, don't stop the progress. Keep going. There's no reason to lead a "settle for" life. Don't settle for just living normally emotionally. Unless you unnecessarily and foolishly attach to the belief that you are unable to do it, there's no reason that you cannot live well emotionally. There's no good reason not to transform emotional normalcy into emotional well-being. Don't worry: there are books like this one and guides, perhaps including me, who can help you do that.

In fact, if you are ripe for it, you may be astounded at how quickly that can occur. The more determined you are to diminish or eliminate emotional suffering, the more motivation you have to do it. That's the consolation hidden within what might be almost suicide-inducing emotional suffering. After you finish reading this book and absorbing the ideas presented here, how fast might you be able to dissolve *any* negative emotion that is troubling you? It may take just an hour or two! Even if it were to take you a day or two or even a week, so?

The real value of learning about emotions isn't having improved thoughts: it's using that improved thinking to improve the quality of our emotional lives.

There's an added important benefit in addition to the obvious one of reducing or eliminating emotional suffering: mastering emotions will give you practical experience with respect to what is required for mastering life. **Mastering emotions is a gateway to mastering life**.

"In order to swim, one takes off all one's clothes – in order to aspire to the truth, one must undress in a far more inward sense, divest oneself of all one's inward clothes, of thoughts, conceptions, selfishness, etc., before one is sufficiently naked."
--Soren Kierkegaard

When you are ready to strip down, please continue.

1

Emotional Dissatisfaction

Living well emotionally (flourishing emotionally, enjoying emotional freedom) is the opposite of living poorly emotionally (suffering emotionally). To live less-than-well emotionally is to experience emotional dissatisfaction. If, as is unlikely, you are already living well emotionally, there's no need for you to be reading this. If, as is likely, you experience more than mild, occasional emotional dissatisfaction, *it's possible for you to do better emotionally for the rest of your life.* Furthermore, doing so doesn't necessarily require any more time or effort than emotional bondage, and it usually takes much less.

In fact, doing so is not only possible, but, as I explain in what follows, it's simple. You may never have encountered that idea before and, even if you have, you may not believe it. However, it's true and I hope to convince you of its truth in what follows.

Whether positive or negative, **emotions disrupt peace of mind**. They are disturbances. Positive emotions are reactions to situations that we take to be good for us; negative emotions are reactions to situations that we take to be bad for us.

Emotions are relatively intense evaluative judgments. That's sufficient to prime the pump. Before considering it, though, let's quickly review some facts about emotions to ensure that your expectations are realistic.

To experience an emotion is typically, if it's positive, to ride the emotional roller coaster up and, if it's negative, to ride the emotional roller coaster down. Usually, but not always, experiencing a negative emotion is an unpleasant downer, whereas experiencing a positive emotion is a pleasant upper.

Emotions are natural. They evolved because they are useful. One important way that they are useful is that they sometimes stimulate life-saving behaviors in emergency situations. Even negative emotions like fear, even though they are unpleasant to experience, can have good or beneficial consequences. It's natural, for example, to jump back without thinking as soon as you realize that you are too close to a puff adder. Since living well requires living and since emotions can help us keep living, it's good that we are emotional. So, even if it were possible, your goal with respect to emotions should not be to eliminate them.

When you experience an emotion that you like, there's no need to eliminate it. On the other hand, when you experience an emotion that you don't like, it would be good to understand how to eliminate it. You'll understand why that's possible for you to do by the time you finish reading this book.

That's the **practical goal** that I have for you. I am confident that you can do it because I myself have done it. In fact, I hope that you are able to do it much more quickly than I was able to do it. I had no guide to flourishing emotionally and needed to figure everything out for myself.

Permit me to introduce myself as your guide. I'm a philosopher, a lover of wisdom, with over half a century of experience as a philosopher. I'm a former member of MENSA and have a doctorate in philosophy. I taught philosophy (and humanities) full-time for 32 years to undergraduates. I'm the author of 28 books. I've practiced zen meditation daily for over 22 years. I have read, studied, and taught all the major philosophers in the eastern philosophic tradition as well as all the major philosophers in the western philosophical tradition. For example, some western philosophers who have had interesting ideas about emotions are Aristotle, the Stoics, Augustine, Descartes, Rousseau, Hobbes, Spinoza, Hume, Kant, Nietzsche, James, Whitehead, and Sartre. Of course, I've also read works by other thinkers like Freud and Jung (who, incidentally, was influenced by Hindu philosophers) as well as poets and novelists, who are not usually classified as philosophers, as well.

My intention in this book is to shorten your learning curve. It would be way beyond the scope of this work to present and evaluate all the major theories about emotions. It really doesn't matter much whether or not you ever become a master thinker with respect to emotions; what matters is only whether or not you enjoy emotional well-being. I present here my conclusions about emotional well-being. My hope is that they will enable you to live well emotionally much, much, much more quickly than would otherwise be possible.

My grounding is squarely in the tradition stretching from ancient philosophers such as Plato and Aristotle to such recent philosophers as Wittgenstein, Sartre, and Robert C. Solomon who think that philosophy should be useful. The point of studying it is to improve the quality of our thinking so that we may improve the quality of our lives. The word 'philosopher' means 'lover of wisdom.' A successful philosopher is someone who has become wise and lives well.

The most important human creation is not a theory or a book or a work of art or an invention or anything like that; instead, it's a well-lived life itself.[3] For literally thousands of years, philosophers have concerned themselves with emotional well-being because it's important with respect to living wisely or well. If you are troubled emotionally, it doesn't make much difference how good your health is, how great a family you have, how excellent your work is, how famous you are, how fine your house is, and so on. **Emotions are important with respect to living well**.

There are many kinds of emotions. There are different systems for categorizing emotions. There is no one system that is universally accepted for categorizing emotions. Since emotions are subjective experiences, that's not surprising.

Some scientists study emotions objectively, from the behavioral or third-person [he, she or it] point of view rather than the first-person singular [I] point of view. Obviously, such studies can only be indirect (as scientists readily admit), but, nevertheless, they can be useful.

Paul Ekman is one such scientist who studies faces, particularly micro-expressions, to learn about the underlying emotions that they express. His research establishes that "seven emotions each have a distinct, universal, facial expression: sadness, anger, surprise, fear, disgust, contempt, and happiness."[4] Actually, each of those seven is really a genus with multiple species. For example, anger can range in strength from mere annoyance to outright rage and there can be different types, too, such as cold anger, resentful anger, indignant anger, and so on. For example, happiness covers contentment, excitement, relief, wonder, and bliss. Similar remarks apply to the other five emotional genera.

It's well understood that universally, in other words, across human cultures, emotions prompt physical action. They are motivators. Fear, for example, prompts the impulse either to freeze, to fight, or to flee. Sadness prompts a withdrawing slump in posture as well as loss of overall muscular tone (without other action). Emotions wouldn't be useful unless they were disturbances, unless they disrupted peace of mind and prompted us to act.

What's less well understood is that emotions prompt evaluations of whatever the present situation is that are consistent with the emotion being experienced. To be angry, for example, is, in part, to be predisposed to understand what is happening in a way that justifies and maintains the anger. In that sense, they reinforce themselves. They also reinforce themselves when they are frequently repeated so that they become conditioned reactions.

Emotions that prompt physical actions and evaluations are involuntary. When we are emotional, they are inescapable in the sense that we are unable simply to drop them. They are not deliberate choices and we may not even be aware of them. After it's been stimulated, the goal of instantly escaping the effects of the cascade of hormones that intense emotions stimulate is impossible.

Are emotions experienced in isolation? Usually not. Emotions only infrequently occur singly in isolation.[5] Typically, they are blended together and feed on each other. Identifying a single emotion being experienced is difficult for many people (particularly men in our culture), but disentangling and identifying multiple emotions being experienced can be difficult for anyone.

This explains how just one serious negative emotion can be so devastating. It can be compounded into having more hurtful consequences. Suppose, for example, that my lover dumps me. Suppose that she lived with me for years. It's not as if she died; instead, she rejected me after getting to know me really well. She threw out any meaning or value our past together had and any meaning or value our future together might have had. As I dwell on that, my sadness rises to the level of intense grief. I feel twice as bad when I remember that other women, too, have rejected me. Then I might make things worse by getting angry at myself for being so sad. The anger and sadness compound each other. My anger increases the more I think about it. Anger is the most dangerous emotion. I am ready to punish and retaliate. Maybe she's right; maybe I'm worthless. Maybe I should direct my anger against myself. By some such process I might become suicidal or homicidal.

This is why *learning how to dissolve even just one unwanted emotion in isolation is a powerful tool for living better*. Once you learn how to do that, and I explain how in what follows, you will have armed yourself with a very valuable tool for living better.

We are not only born with some unlearned, involuntary emotional responses, but we continue to learn emotional responses throughout life. When a new emotional response has been learned, it, too, becomes involuntary. This does not entail, however, that we cannot manage learned emotional responses. Furthermore, there's no reason why learned emotional responses cannot be unlearned and, in fact, some scientists believe that that's a practical option.

These, then, are sufficient reminders of some of the everyday facts about our emotional lives.

Let's turn our attention toward the critical idea of emotions as appraisals.

2

The Nature of an Emotion

Emotions require nearly instantaneous appraisals.

The claim that these appraisals are nearly instantaneous does not necessarily entail that they are beyond our control. There's no reason it's impossible to learn how to pay greater attention to them as they are happening. If so, there's no reason why those appraisals cannot be modified, which is exactly what those who live well emotionally are able to do.

We have reached the point where clarity becomes critical. If you don't understand clearly what emotional well-being is and how it's possible, you'll be less likely even to attempt to improve the quality of your emotional life. Our goal is the practical one of enabling you to enjoy abiding emotional well-being.

The critical point about emotional well-being relates to emotions as appraisals. In an attempt to state it with unusual clarity, permit me to regiment ordinary language. Please exercise some patience as I do so. Trust me: the improvement in understanding will be worth it.[6]

Let's agree that an "**object**" (form, thing) is anything that can be singled out for attention, whether or not it is real or taken to be real. (It can be perceived, remembered, imagined, or conceived. For example, your right hand is a perceptual object as is your shirt and your bed. Since remembered objects were usually perceptional and since imagined objects are usually constructed from perceptual qualities, perceptual objects are more fundamental than either remembered or imaginary objects. With respect to conceptual objects such as numbers – not numerals – there's controversy even about whether or not they exist. So a paradigmatic object is perceptual.) We can use 'x' to stand for some object or other. We either single out objects or we don't. For example, sighted people single out colors and blind people don't.

Let's agree that a "**concept**" is a principle of classification. If you are able to divide (sort, conceptualize, categorize, classify, discriminate) objects into red and not-red, you have the concept of redness, in other words, you understand what it is for something to be red. Similarly, you have the concepts of being a right hand, a shirt, and a bed. A paradigmatic concept is a perceptual quality. We can use 'F' to stand for some concept or other. There are many different conceptual systems because there are many ways to classify objects according to their similarities and differences.

Let's agree that actually to use a concept is to have a "**thought**," in other words to make a judgment or entertain a proposition. If I look at my shirt and think "this is red," then I've had a thought. Of course, not all thoughts are true; it's possible to make mistakes when thinking. Furthermore, not all thoughts are predications, but the other kinds (such as identity judgments) need not concern us here.

Logically, then, there's a clear difference between x [some object or other], F [some concept or other] and x is F [some thought or other].

It's possible to single out an object and not make any judgment about it; it's possible to suspend judgment. This requires, though, at least that that object have one or more qualities because a qualityless object is impossible to single out. It is at the level of objects that our epistemic apparatus makes contact with the world.

However, merely singling out an isolated object is very unusual. Ordinarily, not only do we not suspend judgment, but the ways in which we understand objects become so habitual (familiar, automatic) that they become indistinguishable from the ways in which we single them out. Suppose, for example, that there's a table in your kitchen. When you last entered your kitchen, did you think something like, "There's an object. I notice that it has legs and a flat surface. I wonder what it is. Maybe it's a piece of furniture? Oh, yes, it's a table." Or did you simply see it as a table? My guess is that you simply saw it as a table. If so, that's because you've seen it repeatedly and don't wonder about it at all anymore.

In fact, it often takes an artist to get us to perceive objects in fresh ways, to shock us out of mental ruts. That's true for both descriptive and evaluative judgments. [See below for that distinction.]

Some thoughts we accept as true. Some we don't accept, including those we are unsure about. To have a "**belief**" is to accept or attach to a judgment. For example, if I've no reason to suspect that I'm misperceiving, when I judge that my shirt is red I also naturally believe that it is red. Almost always when we apprehend something we believe what appears to be true. Even though it's nondemonstrative evidence (in other words, insufficient to guarantee truth), even though I could be mistaken, it's my belief [opinion] that my shirt is red simply because I perceive it to be red.

Thoughts and beliefs are of two kinds: descriptive and evaluative. "That is a painting" is a **descriptive** thought that amounts to the claim that that object falls under the concept of being a painting. "That painting is good" is an **evaluative** thought that amounts to the claim that that painting is valuable (preferable, normative). Similarly, "what she did was wrong" is an evaluative judgment that amounts to the claim that her action wasn't right, wasn't a choice that she should have made.

One last distinction is critical before turning to the structure of emotions. We are rational beings. We believe thoughts when we think they are supported by (at least some) evidence. (If you doubt that, try to think of an actual belief of yours that is not supported by any evidence whatsoever.) Often, the evidence we have for believing some thought is insufficient to guarantee its truth. That's the distinction worth considering briefly.

There's a difference between **demonstrative evidence** and **nondemonstrative evidence**. While the latter is taken to provide some grounds for belief, only the former guarantees truth. To have demonstrative evidence is to find mistake in believing some particular proposition inconceivable. Demonstrative evidence and only demonstrative evidence yields certainty, indubitibility. For example, I find it inconceivable that I am mistaken in believing that red is a color or that two and three are five. (It's true that all our statements are corrigible with respect to their linguistic propriety, but let's make that irrelevant by ruling out the possibility that I've mislearned the relevant words.) In other words, I have **knowledge** that red is a color and that two and three are five. These are, in fact, necessarily true beliefs; I'm unable to think of how they could be otherwise.

Do I know that my shirt is red? No I don't. That's just an **opinion.** If it's true at all, it's only contingently true. I'm able to think of how it could be otherwise. I know that it *appears* to be red; about that I cannot think of how I could be mistaken. However, perhaps my vision is deceiving me and, although it appears to be red, perhaps it's not actually red.

Perhaps, to recall the skeptic's dream argument, instead of perceiving a red shirt I am only dreaming that I am perceiving a red shirt. Since it's possible that I'm mistaken that I'm awake, it's possible that I'm wrong in believing that there is a red shirt before me now even though there appears to be one. My dreaming that there is a red shirt before me would provide no evidence at all that there is a red shirt before me. Such dream perceptions lack epistemic worth. Ask yourself seriously: Might I be dreaming now? Well, are you able to imagine waking up a few seconds from now? If so, you do not know that you are now awake. For any putative criterion that you think of for distinguishing perceiving x from dreaming that you are perceiving x, you could dream that that criterion is satisfied when it's not.

Assuming that the skeptic's dream argument is or could be made sound, although I still believe that my shirt is red, I admit that I have only nondemonstrative evidence that it is true. In other words, I've detached sufficiently from my belief to admit that I might be mistaken.

Giving more consideration to perception in that way may enable you to detach more easily from perceptual judgments. If that's difficult for you, it may be because you still are thinking of perceiving as passive. It's not. It's active. Philosophers and scientists have been aware of this for a long time. As William James writes, "Without selective interest, experience is utter chaos."

Is your perceptual experience utterly chaotic? No. Why not? It's because you are taking in perceptual information about the world within a conceptual framework. In other words, perception is not just passive reception but also interpretation. (This is why there's no such thing as a known concrete perceptual fact about reality.)

We live in the domain of becoming, incessant flux or novelty. Novel experiences create uncertainty. Uncertainty creates stress. Stress creates anxiety, which is cognitive static. How can we reduce anxiety? Simple: diminish attention (consciousness, awareness) by narrowing our focus. In fact, that's what our brains do for us all the time even though we are not aware of it.[7]

In other words, perceiving is interactive. **Perceptual beliefs are constructions** even though we are not aware that our brains are doing any construction.

One way this happens is based on the fact that we are able to remember experiences. Scientists who study the processing of perceptual information as well as long-term and short-term memory talk about patterns of relationships of data stored in memory that some call "schema." If stored perceptual information were disorganized, our memories would be much less efficient. We are able to form schemas quickly to organize information better, but, once formed, schemas resist change.

For us, notice two important takeaways. First, memorial data is interconnected, in other words, one thought leads to another. It's as if isolated thoughts are anathema and must immediately be given a family. Second, this interconnected data influences perception, which explains our well-known tendency to perceive only what we expect to perceive. New perceptual information is assimilated to existing schemas. If we encounter perceptions that are unexpected in the sense that they don't fit our expectations, we have great difficulty processing and assimilating that data. So we miss even accurate information just because it fails to conform to our preconceptions.

Furthermore, there's a critically important concept that recent studies have confirmed has an enormous impact on our judgments, namely, our self concepts. Daniel Goleman goes so far as to say that "Memory is autobiography."[8] In other words, egocentricity pervades our judgments. The ego is a censor incessantly busy selecting, distorting, and deleting perceptual information. It's a chief source of resistance to learning. *We all have egocentric biases and cognitive blinds spots* – and they evolved because they can be beneficial, in other words, they often help us to survive and reproduce. When the ego admits information that is threatening to it, that can affect self-esteem and lead to depression, which diminishes the chances of evolutionary success. Nevertheless, in terms of making evaluations and decisions about how to live, obviously cognitive bias or blindness can be extremely harmful. Those who fail to live examined lives are more prone to experience their ill effects.

Ego attrition is the process of diminishing the power of the ego. It's simple in theory, but it's difficult in practice. However, it can be very valuable for two reasons. First, it leads to more accurate perceptional judgments. The more accurate our perceptions, the less deluded we are. The less deluded we are, the better our decisions about how to be and what to do are likely to be. In the Buddhist tradition, the cure for delusion is panna, which means "insight." It's the ability to perceive reality as it is. Second, it also leads to enhanced emotional flourishing. Why? The less personally we take things, the better we feel.

So **neither our perceptions nor our memories are sources of knowledge**. At best, all nonconceptual perceptual or memorial judgments are opinions and, so, might be false.[9] When it comes to opinions, I encourage you to keep in mind what Voltaire said: "Doubt is not a pleasant state, but certainty is a ridiculous one."

You may be wondering, "What does any of this have to do with emotional well-being?" Good question. It does seem too theoretical to have much to do with emotional well-being. I show its relevance in what follows. It's required to understand how emotional well-being is possible. It's critical to understand how it's possible, even just in theory, how an unwanted emotion can be dissolved quickly.

3

Emotional Evaluation

S uppose that when you spoke with your mother on the telephone yesterday she told you that she was feeling fine. Suppose, however, that she died in her sleep last night and you haven't learned yet of her death.

How do you feel about that? What emotion, if any, are you experiencing?

Of course, those are trick questions. Since you don't yet realize that she's dead, there's nothing related to her death that would generate any emotions in you. By way of contrast, once you learn of her death, you may experience intense sadness, grief.

What is an emotion?

Emotions have a structure composed of three non-emotional parts. The argument just given reveals the

first part, namely, **a belief about reality, acceptance of some situation taken to be real**. Unless we (either correctly or incorrectly) apprehend some relevant situation, there's nothing to be emotional about.

The objects of emotions are nothing but ordinary objects apprehended through our conceptual filters.[10] In that sense, they are indirectly apprehended. [I return to this critical point in what follows.] The objects of emotions are real or, at least, taken to be real. They are everyday situations (circumstances, facts, states of affairs, events).

There's no such thing as an empty emotion, an emotion that isn't about something. *Emotions are always about particulars*. Unless you believe that your mother died, it's impossible to be emotional about her death.

Permit me four clarifying points about this first element of emotions.

First, apprehensions about reality are sometimes indistinguishable from misapprehensions. Mis- apprehensions can be as believable as apprehensions, which is why sometimes we believe what is false and experience wholly inappropriate emotions. This may happen when we suffer from illusions or delusions. An *illusion* occurs when we misunderstand something we perceive. For example, a child who hears creaking under his bed may take it to be the sound of a ghost and become frightened. An adult hearing the same sound may instead correctly attribute it to the settling of the house and have no emotional reaction to it at all. A *delusion* occurs when we take something that isn't real to be real. If the "sound" the child heard came from his fevered imagination rather than the creaking house, he was suffering from a delusion.

Millennia ago philosophers noticed that there may be no intrinsic difference between veridical (true) perceptions and nonveridical (false) perceptions. We should **be humble** when it comes to perceptual beliefs; instead of fanatically attaching to them, it's wise to keep an open mind by always only accepting them tentatively. Believing them is always somewhat risky. We often assume, however, that we know more than we actually do.

Second, and this point has critical practical importance, even beliefs that are grounded in veridical perceptions are never the whole truth. In fact, no judgment, and therefore, no belief, is ever the whole truth. Why? Recall the discussion in the previous chapter that all judgments (and therefore all beliefs) require using concepts, which are principles of classification. **Concepts are inherently partial**. Any putative concept that didn't sort objects wouldn't be a concept at all.

Therefore, it's logically impossible that any judgment could be wholly true. At best a judgment is partially true. In other words, **all judgments are perspectival.**

That's why **the wise never attach wholeheartedly to any thought**. It cannot be the whole truth. Only fools permit themselves to be fanatically attached to thoughts. This provides the justification for the claim that unwanted negative emotions may be quickly dissolved: that occurs when the beliefs upon which they depend come to be considered false.

(The best that can be done using language would be something like: 'thus!' Of course, such an ejaculation does not even appear to state a truth.[11])

Third, unreal (nonexistent) objects can be as causally efficacious as real objects when it comes to stimulating emotions. Even if there isn't a ghost under his bed, the child may still fear it.

Fourth, it's helpful to distinguish moods from emotions. A "**mood**" is a generalized emotion. A mood may be about no particular object. Whereas the child may fear the ghost, it's possible to be, for example, anxious about nothing in particular or about one's whole world or surreality. Similarly, one could be euphoric, depressed, or melancholy. Moods and emotions are not cleanly divisible. They reinforce each other and blend into each other. Because this is so, learning how to dissolve an unwanted emotion can also be effective in dissolving a powerful unwanted mood.

The **second** part of an emotion is really an emendation upon the first part. Here's a simple way for me to lead you to it:

Quick – how do you feel about the fact that it's raining right now in Tokyo? Just suppose for the sake of the example that it's true that it's raining right now in Tokyo. What emotion are you experiencing about that?

Unless you happen to be in Tokyo and have some reason to care one way or the other, you undoubtedly have no feelings about that situation at all.

It's this second part of an emotion that's the critical part: *unless a situation is apprehended as relevant to our lives in some way, we'll have no emotional reaction to it* at all. If the rain in Tokyo doesn't matter to you, you simply won't have any feelings about it. What makes an emotion different from an ordinary apprehension is that it's a kind of **evaluative apprehension**. The judgment "*this is good for me*" is the essence of every positive emotion and the judgment "*this is bad for me*" is the essence of every negative emotion. It's only when we relate some situation to ourselves that we *ever* experience an emotion. It's only when we take situations to be *self-involved* that we ever experience an emotion. Now that it's been pointed it out, that may well seem obvious.

As one recent philosopher states, emotions "are not concerned with *the* world but with *my* world. They are not concerned with 'what is really the case' with 'the facts,' but rather with what is *important.*"[12] While usually present, the **third** part of an emotion is sometimes missing. What is it? It's the bodily feeling or **physiological sensatio**n or set of sensations that typically accompany the self-involved evaluations. Different emotions feel differently. For example, anger and sadness may be felt in different parts of the body.

Furthermore, according to Ekman, "each individual's emotional experience is unique."[13] Different people may feel the same emotional differently. I may experience anger in my throat and you may experience it in your gut. Furthermore, different emotions are accompanied by different desires. For example, when we are angry, we want to punish; when we are sad, we want to regain what's been lost. We differ emotionally in terms of the "speed of emotional onset, strength of emotional response, duration of the emotional response, and how long it takes to recover."[14]

A good way to think about this third part is to realize that, although we often separate mind (thoughts) from body, those two can be understood as one entity, a bodymind or mindbody. An emotion requires such nonseparation. It's a connection between the two.

If the connection is weak, if the thought involved seems of very little value, there will be no noticeable change in the body. An emotion is certainly not just a bodily feeling or sensation. Most such feelings are indifferent to our beliefs; they can occur without any self-involved judgment at all. Also, we may claim that, for example, we can be angry for a sustained period without actually feeling angry for most of that time.

By the way, please realize that I did not invent this analysis of emotions. It's not original with me. I learned it from others and accepted it only after I tested it against my own experience.

Now that you have learned it, please test it against your own experience. For example, recall the last powerful emotion you experienced or one that you are experiencing now. Does it not involve *an apprehension of a situation that you take to be real as well as a belief that that situation is either good or bad for you?* Please test it for yourself based on your own experience. Because understanding emotional well-being depends upon this analysis, it's important that you accept it (or, perhaps, replace it with a better one). Once you do, you are ready for the important step.

Has the big idea occurred to you yet? The critical practical point about how to end emotional suffering follows from the analysis just given. Are you able to think of it on your own? I encourage you to stop reading right now and think hard about that for a while.

4

Emotional Well-Being

A change in the relevant beliefs typically changes the feeling, the third part (if any) of an emotion.

A change in the initial part, the belief about reality, also changes the emotion. If that belief turns out to be mistaken, then the emotion disappears. Once you realize that what you are seeing in the dim light is a rope rather than a snake, your fear will quickly vanish. Without a self-involved situation to be about, there is no emotion. Unlike a snake, a rope will never attack you.

There's more. This is the big idea that has critical practical importance: **a change in the relevant evaluation changes the emotion itself.** Again, an emotion's essence (whatness) requires a self-involved evaluation that is believed about whether some situation taken to be real is good or bad for us.

Please let that soak in for a moment. Are you having an "aha" moment?

Suppose you are suffering from a powerful unwanted emotion. How, in principle, is it possible to put an end to that suffering? Simple: **Change the relevant belief!** Detach from it. Let it go. Stop clinging to it.

It's not enough to believe that's possible in general. What is required to dissolve a particular emotion is actually focusing on that emotion and doing it.

Once you understand what needs to be done, how to do it, and practice doing it, you'll realize that it's just another *skill*. If you are serious about living well emotionally, you'll master it; if not, you won't.

At first, you'll have to think about using that skill. You may even forget to use it if your emotional situation isn't too disruptive. You'll feel awkward at first. That's alright: you must let yourself feel uncomfortable. That discomfort won't last. Just persist. Once you do, dissolving unwanted emotions will become more and more natural. Practicing will become easier and easier. After a while, it will seem almost as automatic and easy as it is quick. Zig Ziglar: "Anything worth doing is worth doing poorly, until you learn to do it well."

Wisdom is to be practiced, not merely understood. **Unlived wisdom is useless**.

Is it better to live in emotional slavery or emotional freedom? The wise live in emotional freedom. Unlike those in emotional bondage, whenever an emotion arises, they have the choice whether or not to indulge in it. If they don't want it, they can quickly get rid of it.

There was a clear example of this when my Zen teacher's father died. I'm a formal student of The Rev. Bodhin Kjolhede, Roshi. One time in the middle of a week-long zen retreat (<u>sesshin</u>) I attended he left abruptly and didn't return. He explained later that his father had died and he flew out to Arizona for the funeral and to be with his mother and sisters for a few days. What I vividly recall was his telling us that, even though his father was old and had been ill, even though he had understood that the time of his father's death was drawing closer, he was surprised that his emotional equilibrium was so disrupted by that death. He reported that it took him 2 days to return to normal.

It's not that those who live well emotionally never become victims of emotions. That's possible, but, it's more likely that they may still suffer emotionally upon occasion. However, when they do, their emotional suffering is mild and they quickly return to normal. It reminds me of those bottom-heavy, blow up toys for children that return upright as soon as they are knocked over. Emotional health is like physical health: it's not that there's never any ill health but that there's always a fast recovery.

You, too, can learn to enjoy emotional well-being for the rest of your life. In fact, you have already begun to do what is required by beginning to understand how that's possible.

Let's next ensure that you have understood the big idea correctly and thoroughly detached from the most important, common false beliefs about emotions. There are half a dozen such beliefs that need to be undermined. Let's name them "myths" and single them out for attention. They may not be the only false beliefs about emotions that are common, but destroying them will complete the process of opening up for you the realistic possibility that you, too, can flourish emotionally.

5

The Myth of Passivity

The myth of passivity is the idea that we must be passive whenever we experience emotions that we don't want. Supposedly, emotions pass over us without our consent rather like weather fronts. There's simply nothing we can do about them other than to endure them.

All myths are servants of the ego. The myth of passivity is particularly vicious because, when taken to be true, it undermines the very possibility of emotional well-being.

It's easy to understand its purpose, namely, to cast us in the role of helpless martyrs whose only choice is to die or to endure until the storm passes. Supposedly, attempting to battle such powerful forces may be noble, but it's always as fruitless as trying to kill a hurricane with a sword.

Fortunately, that's all hogwash. If your passions ever again threaten to render you passive, please reread this book.

Why is this myth false? It's because, like judgments, **beliefs are actions**. To believe is to do something, namely, to accept a judgment as true.[15] Since you now understand the analysis of emotions, you also understand that there can be no emotions without beliefs.

Who is doing the believing?

Well, we do. I know that I do and, unless your mind works in some dramatically different way than mine does, you do, too.

In other words, we are responsible for our beliefs. We can change them. It's always possible at least to suspend judgment.

Our everyday thoughts and language are seriously infected by the myth of passivity. Supposedly, we are, for example, *paralyzed* by fear as if we were quadriplegics. We are *distracted* by sadness as if someone were playing a musical instrument loudly in the next room. We are *driven* by anger as if someone were poking us with a cattle prod. We are *plagued* by disgust as if by a swarm of locusts. And so on and on.

The way that we think and speak matters to the quality of our lives. Words and conceptualizations matter. As the great philosopher David Hume put it, "there are many positive advantages, which result from an accurate scrutiny into the powers and faculties of human nature."[16]

Since inaccuracy in thought and speech undermines the quality of our lives, it's wise to choose our words about emotions carefully lest we unintentionally obstruct ourselves from living better emotionally.

Before reading this, you may not have taken responsibility for the quality of your emotional life. That may not have been your fault. After all, ignorance about emotions is ubiquitous. There's no justification for feeling bad about that.

Now, though, it's time for **emotional maturity**. Even though you may not think that emotions are completely voluntary, it's nevertheless time to step up and own yours. Why? Again, without the beliefs for which you are responsible you wouldn't have any emotions. If you happen never yet to have done so, it's time to accept responsibility for the quality of your own emotional life.

Incidentally, doing so is not only liberating but it's the opposite of being selfish. For example, the more you work on yourself, the better lover you may be. Love is giving; it's not taking. One way the emotionally immature try to take from others is by using others to make themselves feel better emotionally. Being emotionally mature and loving go with selflessness.[17]

6

The Myth of Innocence

People who accept the myth of passivity also often accept the myth of innocence, which is the idea that, prior to critical reflection, our emotions are valuable because they are free and natural.

As the philosopher Robert Solomon points out, this myth is even enshrined in The Bible: "the more a man knows, the more he has to suffer."[18] That's just false. Innocence is mere irresponsibility and immaturity. **The myth of innocence is simply an excuse.**

What we become emotional about is what we choose to become emotional about. There's nobody else involved when, for example, I become angry or fearful or sad. I'm doing it to myself.

Jean-Paul Sartre: "It is senseless to think of complaining since nothing foreign has decided what we feel . . ."[19]

The great benefit of assuming responsibility is that we gain control. Instead of thinking of ourselves as being buffeted about by blind forces, we take charge of our fates. It's only *after* assuming responsibility that emotional well-being becomes possible. Before then, we are like small children being bullied by life. Now we are able for the first time to take charge of our emotional destinies. It begins to dawn on us that we are free to get off the emotional roller coaster whenever we want.

7

The Myth that Common Tactics Work

The tactics that most people use in an attempt to achieve emotional freedom fail. There are two extreme tactics.

First, there's **ignoring** an emotion. Obviously, this is the easiest tactic to use since it doesn't seem to require doing anything. Furthermore, it can seem to work for weak emotions.

It simply doesn't work, though, for powerful negative emotions. Why? It's impossible not to be aware of what we are trying to ignore. Whenever you experience such an emotion, failing to deal effectively with it may have as its only result the leaking of emotional poison into your life for years.

Yes, it can take years, even decades, for emotional distress to fade. Sometimes it only ends with death. Except for those full of self-hatred, nobody really wants that outcome. Life is short enough already. There's no reason to spoil it with unnecessary emotional suffering.

You have undoubtedly simply tried to ignore a powerful negative emotion. How well did that work? In fact, it doesn't, which is why you've never heard of even a single psychiatrist or clinical psychologist recommending that we ignore powerful negative emotions. No loving mother ever raised her children simply to ignore them.

Facts don't disappear just because we'd like them to disappear. Ignoring a negative emotion is as effective as ignoring cancer. This tactic is so obviously ineffective that it's not worth more discussion.

Second, there's **venting** an emotion, in other words, acting on the basis of it. If, for example, you become very angry with someone, venting might be your choosing to act in an effort to injure or kill that person.

Venting simply doesn't work. As Ekman remarks, venting or "getting your anger out . . . usually makes matters worse."[20]

Notice, though, that even if such an action were carried out, the emotion that prompts it doesn't necessarily dissipate.

Furthermore, venting typically only serves to perpetuate and even strengthen an emotion. Instead of alleviating and eliminating emotional bondage, venting tightens it. After all, we cannot carry on acting out an emotion without continuing to be aware of it.

When you were a child, did your mother teach you to vent negative emotions whenever they bothered you? No loving mother with a working brain would do that. If you were to act that way, you'd wind up in prison.

You've probably already learned for yourself that neither ignoring nor venting are effective at producing emotional tranquility (peace of mind, serenity, emotional well-being). Are there any other common tactics that might work?

Yes, there's one: **taking a time out**. This is what your mother may have taught you. If you started beating on your sister because she accidentally broke one of your favorite toys and you became angry, your mother should have stopped that venting behavior. Furthermore, since she also didn't want you simply to ignore what happened, she may have had you take a time out.

Taking a time out is a much better response than either venting or ignoring. At least if the emotion isn't too intense, sitting in a corner may give you enough time to cool down. So it's an important step in the sense that it avoids either of the two extreme reactions.

By itself, however, it doesn't work. If your emotion is powerful enough, instead of cooling off, you may simply reinforce it by thinking about it. Furthermore, what lesson does it teach? You may avoid making a situation worse by avoiding venting, but, except for that, what's to be learned? It teaches nothing about actually dissolving the negative emotion.

However, it's related to the best tactic that most adults know how to use to deal with negative emotions. As an adult, what do you typically do to try to turn a negative emotion into a positive outcome? Let's turn to the best ordinary alternative.

8

The Sublimation Myth

The idea of sublimation is the hopeful idea of rising above a bad situation to make better. With respect to negative emotions, it's the only common way to make something beneficial out of something distressing. How? It's by trying to transform a negative emotion into a positive accomplishment.

You've also likely tried this. When you last became angry, instead of trying futilely to ignore your anger or lashing out at what you took to be the cause of your anger, did you instead go for a run, do some weight lifting, or clean your house furiously? If so, you were sublimating your anger. Good for you. You tried to turn a negative into something positive. When you were finished exercising or cleaning, that physical activity itself also might have provided you with some satisfaction.

However, since it did nothing directly to cure the underlying emotion, sublimating cannot yield emotional well-being. Still, it's a noble failure.

Is there anything else in addition to sublimation that ordinarily helps?

There's one technique worth mentioning. It's based on the fact that powerful negative emotions are bodily. It's not really surprising, then, that taking good care of our bodies does set up more favorable conditions for emotional flourishing. A healthy brain is required for flourishing emotionally.

For that reason, whenever you find yourself suffering emotionally, I recommend that you take extra good care of your body even though you won't feel like it. That means eating well, exercising well, and getting sufficient rest or sleep. (I've written in multiple other places on how to do each of those well.) That, by itself, probably won't work well in terms of alleviating your emotional distress, but it may help and it certainly won't hurt.

What can help even more is getting clear about what it really means to live well emotionally. Frankly, even many great philosophers seem confused. For example, consider Aristotle. He notes that it's easy, for example, to get angry and anyone can do it. However, getting angry at "the right person, in the right amount, at the right time, for the right end, and in the right way is no longer easy, nor can everyone do it."[21] The idea that there is a right way to get angry is wildly off the mark. Sages who flourish emotionally never get angry. It's incoherent to think that someone could simultaneously be a slave to anger while enjoying emotional well-being, which is liberation from unwanted emotions.

In general, it's the great eastern philosophers, starting with the Axial Age Hindu and Buddhist sages, who are wiser than the great western philosophers when it comes to understanding what it means to flourish emotionally and how to uncover emotional freedom.

9

The Myth of the Irrationality of Emotions

My own serious quest to flourish emotionally included a revealing episode concerning the supposed irrationality or senselessness of emotions.

My beloved wife of fourteen years dumped me in favor of someone else. Soon thereafter I had occasion to speak to a clinical psychologist about my emotional distress. Near the end of the only one-on-one session I booked with her, I asked her for some reading suggestions so that I could teach myself how to do better emotionally. She replied in all sincerity that she couldn't do that because, since emotions are irrational, there's no rational theory about them. Balderdash!

Nietzsche mocks the view that emotions are irrational: "As if every passion did not have its quantum of reason--"[22] There's no such thing as an irrational emotion. Emotions evolved for perfectly intelligible reasons. They all have rational explanations.

It doesn't follow that in some specific situation an emotion is always appropriate. Sometimes, too, emotions are too intense or too weak to be effective.

However, the idea that they are irrational is false. I simply ask you to consult your own experience about this. Whenever, for example, you have found yourself very sad or angry or disgusted, wasn't there something that you took to have stimulated your emotion? Wasn't there some situation that you believed that made you sad, angry, or disgusted? Of course there was. Emotions don't just happen for no reason whatsoever. They are not floating randomly out there in the world like germs that occasionally attack and infect us.

If what you believed was false or otherwise mistaken, your sadness, anger, or disgust were not warranted. However, there is always a reason why we feel the emotions that we feel.

This takes us to the brink of understanding and rejecting the myth that, by itself, is able to obstruct flourishing emotionally for most people.

10

The Situations Myth

D o you believe that *situations cause your emotions?* Most people seem to believe that.

How many times have you yourself thought or said something like, "She made me so angry!" or "I was really saddened by his death" or "That's disgusting!" or "Their winning the championship surprised me"? How many times have you heard others make similar remarks? It happens frequently.

The situations myth is the idea that your situation is causing your emotion.

It's almost certain that you were raised to believe it. Once we accept the ideas that we are unhappy and that our situations are causing our unhappiness, we naturally devote a lot of attention and effort into improving our situations. Because most of us think like that, we spend a lot of the time and energy of our lives trying to make situations more favorable for us.

Answer honestly: How much of your life have you devoted to achieving goals that you thought would make you happy? How has that worked out? Have you spent most of your waking life trying to gain what you think will make you happier? Have you spent a lot of life trying to lose whatever you think is making you unhappy or trying to avoid whatever you think will make you unhappy?

Following the Buddha, I call this "the way of the world," which is a grave mistake for anyone who wants to live well.

The Buddha said, "Don't follow the way of the world."[23] Why did he give us that advice?

It's because it doesn't work. If you want to live well, if you really want to be happy, the worst way to live is to follow the way of the world, which is trying to lose or avoid whatever you don't want and to gain whatever you do want. Notice how this resonates with the second essential feature of emotions that is their essence, namely, either "This is good for me" or "This is bad for me."

Situations happen. A given situation is either real or unreal. All nonsubjective **situations are emotionally neutral**. Any specific situation can be thought about either positively or negatively.

If so, where do their supposed goodness or badness come from? From us of course.

Once this is understood, it's easy to justify. Did the Yankees winning the pennant again make you happy? Well, no. Otherwise their winning the pennant would also have made others happy. Did it? Well, no. If you were happy after they won it, that was because you wanted them to win. You valued and preferred that outcome. By way of contrast, fans of the losing team didn't, which is why they experienced sadness rather than happiness when the Yankees won it again.

Emotions are not caused by such "external" situations. We create emotions by projecting our preferences onto the world and then being in bad faith with ourselves about them. **There would be no emotions without our beliefs**. Don't you have beliefs (thoughts, reasons) that explain why you make decisions as you do? Similarly, you have beliefs creating your emotions. The fundamental idea here should now be clear: **To stop suffering from an emotion, stop accepting the belief that is propping up that emotion.** The egoic mind will resist this, but it will do so only by marshalling other thoughts, which, too, you may stop believing.

If you are unhappy, it's because you decide to be unhappy. If you want to be happy, it's because you decide to be happy. Abraham Lincoln: "Most men are about as happy as they make up their minds to be."

Again, we are responsible for our emotions. Again, despite appearances, this is good news. Why?

It's because we control them. We control them because we are responsible for our thoughts and beliefs, which, again, are actions. Therefore, **the degree of our emotional freedom is up to us.**

It immediately follows that **emotional suffering is optional.** It's independent of situations.

Especially if they are unfamiliar to you, you may resist accepting these ideas. That's perfectly understandable. However, if you want to improve the quality of your emotional life, it's foolish not to question and undermine the psychological momentum of your old ideas about emotions.

It certainly *seems* that situations create emotions. Suppose, for example, that you worked hard for years as a high school student because you desired acceptance from a particular university. Suppose that you achieved that goal. When you read the acceptance letter, you instantly became very happy. Didn't that acceptance create your euphoria?

Actually, taking a closer look reveals an important insight. Human beings are essentially similar. Of course, there are individual differences, but we all want to be happy (to flourish, to thrive, to live well) and, so, we all act in ways that we think will make us happy.

Does reading a college acceptance letter addressed to you cause happiness? If so, why wouldn't anyone else reading such a letter become happy? It's easy to imagine the opposite happening.

Suppose that another student read a similar letter. Suppose that she wanted to go to college B; however, her parents both had graduated from college A and would only pay for her going to college B if she failed to gain admittance to their alma mater, college A. She reads the acceptance letter from A and becomes sad because she knows that it means that she won't be able to afford to attend the college where she wants to go.

College A was also the one that accepted you. So, you read the acceptance letter from A and became happy, whereas she read the acceptance letter from A and became sad. If the letter itself caused the emotion, why would it cause opposite emotions in two different people?

When you heat water, it doesn't sometimes cause the water to boil and at other times cause it to freeze.

The answer is that it wasn't the letter itself that caused the opposite emotions; instead, it was the relevant beliefs. Since you thought "this is good for me," you became happy; since she thought "this is bad for me," she became sad. Same situation, opposite emotional outcomes. The situation itself was emotionally neutral. *It's our interpretations of situations that create emotions – and those interpretations, which are our thoughts or beliefs, are up to us. Drop them and we automatically detach from our emotions.*

Living the way of the world is living with the idea of improving our situations to make us happier. That way of living cannot work to attain more than momentary happiness. Why not?

The world is in **incessant flux** (becoming, relentless change, persistent novelty). Even if you happened to be successful in creating what you think would be the perfect situation for you, in the next moment it'd begin to unravel or fall apart and that would take your momentary happiness with it.

Furthermore, even if, impossibly, it didn't almost instantly begin to unravel, you'd undoubtedly begin to live in fear that it soon would and, so, you'd naturally begin worrying about it. In other words, your emotional burden would increase rather than decrease.

Fortunately, we don't have to change the world to be happy; we just need to change what we believe.

If you are still resistant to this new way of thinking about emotions, it's likely because you fear their absence. If so, you are missing a critical insight. That's just ignorance. *If you have never experienced the absence of all emotions, then you simply don't know what it's like.* There'd be no justification for pretending that it would be terrible. (This is an important mistake that even some philosophers like Robert C. Solomon, who otherwise are able to think well about emotions, make.)

In fact, it's quite the opposite. What's it like? Understanding the nature of emotional well-being better is the topic of the next section.

11

Emotional Liberation

As any sage can confirm, emotional well-being means experiencing the abiding serenity, peacefulness, and joy that surpasses conceptual understanding. It's abiding rather than transitory happiness. It's living a life filled with gratitude and love. It's living the way that sages live. To detach from all evaluative apprehensions is automatically to free yourself emotionally.

The ideas that I'm trying to articulate for you have stood the test of time. That doesn't guarantee their truth, but it's certainly suggestive and reassuring.

Hindu proverb: "Conquer your passions and you conquer the world."

The Buddha said:
> "Just as rain pierces
> a poorly roofed house,
> so passion pierces
> an uncultivated mind.
>
> Just as rain cannot pierce
> a well-roofed house,
> so passion cannot pierce
> a well-cultivated mind." [24]

The second of the four bodhisattvic vows in Zen Buddhism is the vow to uproot "endless blind passions."

Sages (successful philosophers or lovers of wisdom, saints) are so uncommon that you may never have actually met anyone who enjoys perpetual emotional well-being. We certainly don't have ordinary words that describe emotional well-being; the best we can do is, for example, to use a phrase such as 'abiding joy' to distinguish it from the ordinary transitory joy that fluctuates with sorrow.

There's a clear reason why living without emotional disturbances is so wonderful, so serene and tranquil, so peaceful and satisfying. It's not just living without emotions that is the key to living well. Here's the missing critical insight: **living without thoughts is the key to living well.**

What?

Permit me quickly to add that this doesn't mean living without awareness or consciousness. Remember that **thoughts are conceptualizations** or judgments that we attach and cling to as we understand, accept, and believe them. Again, thoughts require concepts, which are essentially divisive or dualistic. Concepts separate; **the presence of concepts separates**. Without thoughts, what remains is awareness of unity. **The absence of concepts unifies.** Since it's logically impossible to describe unity (because descriptions require concepts and concepts are essentially non-unitive), there are no words or concepts that can communicate the direct experiencing awareness of unity. *If you have not yet experienced what I'm referring to, then the most important experience possible for human beings awaits you.* It's named and referred to in many ways such as "spiritual awakening" or "realizing one's true nature" or "union with the divine" or "superconsciousness." It's the change of perspective that comes when thoughts temporarily disappear, which is what is required for mastering life, for becoming a successful philosopher or sage. What remains when thoughts temporarily disappear? Direct experience of the present moment. It's our natural state that is indescribably wonderful.

If so, why has it become so uncommon? The answer has a lot to do with the rise of literacy. Our relation to the earthly biosphere has been contaminated by the incessant thoughts arising from the development of written languages.[25] Why is it so beneficial?

It won't even seem to be beneficial until you realize its companion idea, namely, that **separation is the source of all dissatisfaction** (suffering, discontent, misery, unhappiness). This is why we suffer from what we take to be important losses.

To illustrate this, it may be sufficient simply to mention sadness, which has species that range from annoying to agony. As Ekman notes, "Many types of loss can trigger sadness."[26] We become sad when we realize that we have become separated from something and believe that that separation is bad for us. We may become mildly annoyed when we misplace our car key and have to look for it. We may find ourselves in agony when we watch a beloved child die. We can lose a lover, a friend, self-esteem, the admiration of another, health, a body part, a bodily function, and lots of other things as well. The sadness, the dissatisfaction, comes not from the separation itself but from the belief that that separation is bad for us. Again, there's never an emotion without a relevant, self-involved belief.

Similar remarks apply to all other negative emotions such as anger and fear. If there's no separation between the way that we take the world to be and the way that we want the world to be, there cannot be any unwanted emotions.

It should now make sense why **those without thoughts don't suffer emotionally**. Since they are not thinking, they are not experiencing any separation (disunity, division). Since they are not experiencing any separation, they are not dissatisfied emotionally or in any other way. They dwell in unity in the sense that they experience Becoming from Being (rather than not experiencing Being at all or only occasionally experiencing Being from Becoming). How could that be anything other than peaceful, joyous, and satisfying?

So, no thoughts, no separation. No separation, no dissatisfaction.

Once you begin to grasp these important insights, new interpretations of familiar experiences open up. Consider, for example, how happy you feel when you achieve a major goal. Why do you feel so happy? It's not really because you gained something.

It's because you have detached from all the negative thoughts related to that achievement. As one contemporary successful philosopher puts it: "Achieving our goals makes us happy because it eliminates our negative thoughts about a particular circumstance. Achieving our most difficult goals generally corresponds with a stronger, more intense experience of happiness or relief because we suffered for longer periods of time before achieving them."[27] In short, we become happy when we stop making ourselves unhappy.

The more thoughts (and, so, beliefs) we detach from, the more we experience abiding happiness.[28]

Following the philosopher Merleau-Ponty, David Abram thinks there's a natural reciprocity, a wordless silent conversation, a continual interchange, between our bodies and the natural entities that surround us. We are so engaged with our thoughts and words that we fail to notice why we hurt when we are separated from the natural world. What's his evidence? "Whenever I quiet the persistent chatter of words within my head, I find this silent or wordless dance always already going on – this improvised duet between my animal body and the fluid, breathing landscape that it inhabits."[29] It's interesting to note in this regard that recently scientists who study impaired brains (such as those of stroke victims) have discovered that we process written language in different parts of our brains than where we process spoken language.

Similar to Abram's point about what happens when we detach from thoughts, the philosopher Noah Elkrief argues that, when we stop believing the thoughts that create our emotions, we find ourselves aware of the present moment. In other words, when we drop attachment to the unnatural thoughts, we find ourselves living naturally. That's good because "the present moment

. . . is complete peace, happiness, and freedom."[30] No special situation is required for us to detach from our thoughts.[31] When we stop clinging to the thoughts that create emotions by consciously admitting that we don't know that they are true, we automatically stop experiencing the unwanted emotions that those thoughts create.

Furthermore, there's **no need to gain** something else in order to be happy right now. All that is required is detaching from the thoughts that are causing your unhappiness. You can do that right now. There's no need to wait for some better situation to arise in the future. There's no need to wait for Godot; Godot is already here. Please drop any fantasies you have about the future. The more you exercise your imagination about it, the more you are failing to pay attention to the present moment. How could anyone possibly really enjoy the present moment without paying attention to it?

Again, although these ideas may be new to you, there's really nothing new about any of them. Sages have been offering them to us literally for millennia. If you have never encountered them before that's only because of your impoverished educational background. You almost certainly were not educated as a philosopher and taught to think for yourself.

(If you are a teacher or a parent, do you enjoy having children question everything? Most don't. It's only exceptionally good teachers and parents who encourage us to question seriously, to become philosophers. That's unfortunate, because the quality of our questions determines the quality of our lives.)

It does not follow that we should never think. Avoiding all judgments is impossible. Even if it were possible, it would be foolish. Why? We need good thinking to solve our problems.

Perhaps 20% of our thoughts are fresh, helpful, and original. The problem comes with the other 80% that are stale, unhelpful, and actually obstructive. When we think or judge *compulsively*, which is what all non-sages do, we get stuck in our thoughts and then wonder why the world seems so dead and unappealing. We think and, instead of seriously questioning our thoughts, believe what we think, get trapped in our beliefs, and then wonder why we are dissatisfied.

What's required for mastering life? It's **breaking our addiction to compulsive thoughts**. A master thinks, and thinks well, when thinking is required. Otherwise, a master enjoys life directly rather than getting stuck in a filtering network of thoughts.

The reason I'm even mentioning this here is to enable you to begin to understand the difference between the two methods for emotional flourishing mentioned previously, namely, the reactive and the proactive. The reactive method is all about dissolving an unwanted emotion that you have, and the proactive method is all about the nonarising of such emotions in the first place. Sages, those who fully master life, don't experience powerful negative emotions because they have mastered the proactive method. (Again, they may still occasionally experience some milder negative emotions, but they understand how to "cook" them until they vanish in short order.)

You do not have to become a sage to master the reactive method, which is the chief topic of this book. An important reason that I've mentioned sages at all is because **the same practices that can yield emotional well-being can also yield sagehood**. So, rather than doing nothing and staying stuck, you have a choice: you may practice those methods (i) until you're enjoying emotional freedom whenever you want it and stop or (ii) continue using them even after that until unwanted emotions begin to arise less and less frequently.

In either case, what **the reactive method** is should now be clear: *When you find yourself suffering from an unwanted emotion, identify the belief that is causing it. Then admit to yourself that you lack knowledge of its truth. Once you actually detach from accepting it as true (as opposed to merely accepting the general claim that you are ignorant), the emotion that it's causing will quickly vanish.* I summarize this for you into a simple, useful 5 step method below. *Similarly, if, with serious introspection,* *you find yourself suffering from an unwanted emotional state that is caused by multiple emotions, identify the beliefs that are causing them and admit to yourself that you lack knowledge of their truth. Once you actually detach from accepting them as true, the emotional state that they are causing will quickly vanish.*

Using this method successfully requires skill. Like any other important skill, it takes practice to master it. So? Always, one must pay the price. If you are willing to begin practicing and to learn from your mistakes as you do so, you'll soon be enjoying an increasing degree of emotional freedom.

You may wonder if it's *always* possible to detach from accepting thoughts as true. It is. Permit me a concrete example to illustrate the point.

Suppose that you really love your husband and he unexpectedly dumps you for someone younger and more beautiful. You think, "This is bad for me" and instantly find yourself in a torrent of grief.

Do you, however, *know* that this is bad for you? Remember that to know something is to find mistake in believing it inconceivable. Of course you don't know that it's bad for you. Why?

That evaluation depends upon its future consequences. All the future consequences of his dumping you must be known for your belief "this is bad for me" to be justified. You never know all of them because you never even know some of them. It's impossible to know the future, which is unknown and unknowable.

Still, you say, I *believe* that the future consequences will be bad even though my evidence is nondemonstrative. Well, that itself is a mistake. *Since we always lack any evidence of what the future will be like*, you don't have *any* (demonstrative or nondemonstrative) evidence of what it will be like. Future connections may or may not turn out to be like past connections; we always just have to wait and see.[32] You may eventually come to have opinions about some of them, but that's beside the point.

It could be that you'll stay stuck to your grief for years and years. Why would you do that? It could be because you think that that's a good way to demonstrate your love for him and, so, the depth of your loss. In other words, that's just another thought sustaining the grief. It's not necessary for that to happen.

Perhaps his staying with you would have been worse for you. Perhaps the next time when you were to go together to his company's annual Christmas party you'd both have been killed in an automobile accident.

Perhaps his leaving you will be better for you than your life with him would have been. Perhaps you'll quickly meet another man and enjoy a love affair with him that is far better than the one you used to have with your husband.

The future is open to all possibilities. It's un-warranted arrogance to think otherwise. So please admit your ignorance about it and detach from your grief by detaching from your thought that "this is bad for me."

One aid that may help here is to admit that we never experience the future (as future). Experience only ever occurs in the present moment. In that sense, the future never arrives. If it were to be experienced, it would not be future because it would be present. Since it's impossible ever to experience the future, how could we possibly know anything about it? How could we ever have any evidence about it whatsoever?

If we agree that right actions diminish future pain and suffering and wrong actions increase future pain and suffering and that the future is unknown and un-knowable, then it immediately follows that it's impossible to know the difference between a right and a wrong action. The thesis that there is knowledge of right and wrong is an important ethical myth.[33]

Actions always only occur in the present moment. To act is to act now; to fail to act is to fail to act now. The consequences of an action or nonaction are critical for evaluating whether it's right or wrong. Since it's impossible to know what all the consequences of some action that we are considering are, *it's impossible to know what to do.* So, if you have been beating up yourself or others about wrong actions, please stop. We can guess about future consequences, but such deliberation is as limitless as our imaginations. The best procedure for acting rightly is to detach from all thoughts and to rely on our "intuition" or "gut" as a method that gives us the best chance of acting rightly and not acting wrongly. Since emotions essentially involve judgments, this is quite different from venting or doing what emotionally feels right. Actually, it's the way that sages act and, although even they make mistakes, it's the best that we are able to do from a moral point of view.

The key to understanding the plausibility of this is to realize that it requires detachment from one's self concept. Either evaluation that grounds emotions (namely, either "this is bad *for me*" or "this is good *for me*") is all about you. Guess what? Didn't you learn when you were about 4 years old that the purpose of the world had nothing whatsoever to do with making you happy? *Your surreality is all about you, but reality is not all about you.*

Furthermore and much more radically, your self concept, the idea that you are an isolated self separated from the rest of reality, is a delusion. What sages do is to detach from their egocentricity, from their self concepts. They learn how not to suffer from ego delusion. Much of their imperturbability and emotional tranquility comes from the fact that they therefore take nothing personally. **Sages don't mind reality.** It's not that they fail to be fully aware of situations; it's they accept them fully even when they would prefer things to be otherwise than they are and even when they are engaged in trying to make things better.

Ego attrition is hard work, but it's what is required to master life. Detaching from egocentricity is simple, but it's not easy.

After speaking with His Holiness the Dalai Lama, Ekman realized that the right kind of practicing enables some people [sages] to choose not to become emotional or, when emotional, to behave rightly rather than wrongly.[34]

Furthermore, detaching from beliefs has an enormous impact on life. Referring to sages, Ekman notes that "Not everyone imports from their past into current situations emotional scripts that don't really match."[35] It's not just beliefs related to emotions that sages detach from, it's all beliefs. To understand this, ask: "Where do my beliefs come from?" The answer is that you learned them in the past, didn't you?

What happens when, as most of us do, we drag our beliefs from the past into the present moment? We kill the freshness of our experiences. We make our experiences much heavier and more serious. We diminish their spontaneity and our creativity. We continue to be self-absorbed. We retain the tendency to use the present moment as merely a stepping stone to some better future moment. We spoil life.

What happens when, as sages do, we stop dragging our beliefs from the past into the present moment? Our experiences become fresh. As they become lighter, we become more playful and inclined to laugh. We become more creative, more original. When we drop self-absorption, we instantly become more loving. We relax and enjoy life more. We stop trying to use the present moment merely as a stepping stone and delight in its preciousness.

Your relationship with the present situation is what determines the quality of your emotional life. If you detach from your thoughts and beliefs about it, you'll automatically detach from any unwanted emotions about it.

You should now understand how that's possible and why doing it is wise. The benefit of doing so is lasting peacefulness, joy, happiness, and satisfaction. That, not so incidentally, is where genuine love and creativity arise.

Freeing yourself from bondage to unwanted emotions by detaching from relevant thoughts is **the cleverest way to enjoy life**.

That's the theory. What remains, if you want, is to apply these ideas to your own life. Anyone reading this with understanding can do it. Therefore, you now understand what to do. If you have sufficient motivation, if you are sufficiently troubled emotionally, you'll do it.

12

Your Next Step

If you have understood the ideas presented here (and if you are still somewhat unclear and have only read it once, I encourage you to read it again), *you don't need additional theoretical understanding.* You now understand that emotional freedom is possible and why it's possible for anyone. The purpose of improving our understanding is to live better; learning ought not to be a kind of incessant distraction, which is what the ideal of understanding for the sake of understanding is.

Nevertheless, if you want to learn more, there are plenty of readily available books, courses, and videos. You could start searching by keywords on Amazon for books to purchase or on YouTube for videos to watch for free.

My best recommendation, though, is that your time and effort would be better spent *applying these ideas* to your own emotional life. Doing so successfully won't just help you, it will help all those with whom you come in contact; recognizing that, especially when it comes to those you love, can by itself provide sufficient motivation. Fortunately, there are readily available books and teachers who can help you do that. Some tactics you may try don't work. For example, if you simply try to ignore or silence the beliefs that are creating your unwanted emotions, you'll fail. For example, distractions don't work because, once they are done entertaining you, awareness of your unhappiness will again flood your consciousness.

The task is to emerge from what Eckhart Tolle refers to as "the stream of involuntary and incessant thinking" that poisons life.[36] As Tolle points out, and as the Buddha pointed out some 2400 years ago, the fundamental problem is that you identify with your thoughts, which is why you are addicted to thinking. In that sense, **ignorance of your true nature is the real problem**. You don't have to realize your true nature in order to stop suffering emotionally, but it is necessary to realize it if you are to master life and become a successful philosopher or sage.

I thank you for reading this. I congratulate you for beginning to think well about emotional well-being.

I wish you well.

Dennis E. Bradford

Conesus, New York

Endnotes

1. Although I again mention it in the last section, I teach proactive methods in other books as well as in private consultations.
2. The Buddha, <u>The Dhammapada</u> (Tomales, California: Nilgiri, 1985; Eknath Easwaran, tr.), p. 174.
3. I discuss this idea in my <u>ARE YOU LIVING WITHOUT PURPOSE? The Simple Secret Nobody Tells You: How to Eliminate Anxiety</u>.
4. Paul Ekman, <u>Emotions Revealed</u> (N.Y.: Henry Holt, 2007), p. 58.
5. Eckman, p. 70.
6. If you want a more thorough discussion of the following distinctions, I recommend reading my <u>Mastery in 7 Steps</u>. If you are hungry for still more, I recommend reading Butchvarov's <u>The Concept of Knowledge</u>, <u>Being Qua Being</u>, <u>Skepticism in Ethics</u>, and <u>Anthropocentrism in Philosophy</u>.

7. An excellent book on all this is Daniel Goleman, <u>Vital Lies, Simple Truths: The Psychology of Self-Deception</u> (N.Y.: Simon and Schuster, 1985). Another is Richard J. Heuer, Jr., <u>Psychology of Intelligence Analysis</u> that was originally published by the CIA Center for the Study of Intelligence.

8. Goleman, p. 96.

9. There can be, however, conceptual perceptual truths that are necessarily true such as red is a color. I discuss these briefly in <u>Mastery in 7 Steps</u>. For a more thorough discussion, see Butchvarov's <u>The Concept of Knowledge</u>.

10. See also Robert C. Solomon, <u>The Passions</u> (Indianapolis: Hackett, 1993), p. 116.

11. I return to the nature of unconceptualized reality and how we feel when apprehending it in what follows.

12. Solomon, p. 19. His italics.

13. Ekman, p. 232. Cf. p. 153.

14. Ekman, p. 232.

15. Compare Solomon: "An emotion is a *judgment*, something we *do*." (Solomon, p. 125). His italics. He (and I) give Sartre credit for emphasizing this: "Sartre defends a view of the emotions as conscious *acts*, as purposive . . . our emotions are nothing other than our own

choices, views of the world for which we alone are responsible." Robert C. Solomon, "Sartre on Emotions" in Paul Arthur Schilpp, The Philosophy of Jean-Paul Sartre (LaSalle, Illinois: Open Court, 1981), pp. 212 & 227.

16. From Hume's An Enquiry Concerning Human Understanding, section 1.

17. For more on this, see my Love and Respect.

18. The New English Bible, Ecclesiastes 1:19.

19. Quoted by Solomon from Sartre's Being and Nothingness. I couldn't find the quote, but that may be because it's Solomon's own translation.

20. Ekman, p. 120.

21. Aristotle, Nicomachean Ethics 1109a27-8, Terence Irwin, translator.

22. Friedrich Nietzsche, The Will to Power (N.Y.: Random House, 1967; Kaufmann and Hollingdale, trs.), p. 208.

23. The Dhammapada (Easwaran translation), p. 125.

24. The Buddha, The Dhammapada (N.Y.: RandomHouse, 2004; Glenn Wallis, translation), p. 5.

25. By far the best book I've read about this is The Spell of the Sensuous (N.Y.: Random House, 1996) by the philosopher David Abram.

26. Ekman, p. 83.

27. Noah Elkrief, <u>A Guide to The Present Moment</u>, p. 48.
28. I've discussed this in other writings where I refer to it as the opening of Becoming to Being. Becoming is temporal; Being is eternal. Although we may appear only to be temporal beings, the wise are aware that we are eternal as well as temporal.
29. Abram, p. 53.
30. Elkrief, p. 41.
31. Elkrief, p. 161.
32. The classic analysis here was given by Hume in his <u>A Treatise of Human Nature</u>, part 1.
33. I discuss this elsewhere. See my "Beyond Skepticism in Ethics" in Larry Lee Blackman, ed., <u>The Philosophy of Panayot Butchvarov</u> (Lewiston, N.Y.: Edwin Mellen, 2005).
34. Ekman, p. 32.
35. Ekman, p. 41.
36. Eckhart Tolle, <u>The Power of Now</u> (Novato, California: Namaste & New World, 1999), p. xv.

About the Author

D ennis E. Bradford is extremely well-qualified to write about emotional well-being. You have found a guide who has "been there and done that!"

Education and Teaching Experience:

- 58 years experience as a philosopher, a lover of wisdom
- Diploma from Blair Academy
- B. A. in philosophy from Syracuse University
- M. A. and Ph.D. in philosophy from The University of Iowa
- 32 years experience teaching philosophy and humanities as well as counseling undergraduates full-time at the State University of New York College at Geneseo
- Studied and taught all the major philosophers from both the Western and Eastern philosophical traditions
- 26 years daily meditation practice

Publications:

- 29 books [including 6 works of fiction under pen names]
- Multiple articles [including 20 articles at my.ez-inearticles.com]
- Several hundred blog posts on well-being at www.Dennis-Bradford.com
- Multiple websites including: https://endfearfast.com/

Personal Information:

- Former member of MENSA
- Former member of the American Philosophical Association
- Amazon bestselling author
- Many years playing in the Rochester Metro Hockey League
- 2 years as a lieutenant in the U. S. Army with overseas duty in Korea
- Lives peacefully in his home on the shore of a Finger Lake in upstate New York
- Volunteers weekly leading a meditation group at a nearby prison
- Amazon Author Central page: https://www.amazon.com/Dennis-E.-Bradford/e/B0047EI11A/

Fast Start Guide:

Emotional Humility

Here are the 5 steps that work to dissolve any unwanted emotion:

First, assume full responsibility for your beliefs.
Situations do not create your emotions; rather, it's your beliefs, your interpretations about some situations, that create your emotions. You may have no responsibility whatsoever with respect to the reality of the situation, but you – and only you – are wholly responsible for whatever beliefs you have about it. Nobody except you ever decides what your beliefs are.

Second, recall the nature of emotions.
Emotions always have three parts. (i) You believe that some situation is real. (ii) You believe that that situation is bad (or good) for you. (iii) You also have a physiological sensation or set of sensations that accompany

those beliefs. Without the first two components, the third component will be missing, so set it aside.

Third, select a particular unwanted emotion.

The emotion that you select should be the one that you don't want. For example, if you are grieving because you just learned of the death of someone you love, that grief is the emotion that should be selected.

Realize, though, that powerful emotions only infrequently occur in isolation. There may be two or more emotions that need to be disentangled and selected, and it sometimes requires considerable skill to isolate a targeted emotion.

Fourth, critically asses its central belief.

Ask yourself: 'Do I know that that situation is real? Am I certain?' You probably don't know it. However, if you are uncertain, there may be practical steps (such as asking friends) that you can take to verify it.

It's typically more important to ask yourself: 'Do I know that this situation is bad for me? Am I certain?' You *never* know that; it's possible that you are mistaken about it. Why? Even if the situation is real, it doesn't follow that it's bad for you. The evaluation of any situation as good or bad depends upon accurately assessing its consequences. To do that you'd have to know all its consequences. However, since the future is unknown and unknowable, it's impossible to know all its consequences; hence, you can never be sure that some situation will have more bad consequences for you than good ones.

Fifth, detach from it.
Since the belief that that situation is bad is only a hypothesis rather than a known truth and since it's upsetting you, what's the point of sticking with it? Detach from it by admitting that it's uncertain. By continuing to attach to it, all you are doing is continuing to upset yourself. Honestly admit to yourself that you don't really know whether or not its consequences will be, on the whole, more negative than positive for you.

Once you reduce the critical relevant belief back to a mere thought, that negative emotion will soon dissolve completely, especially if you regularly practice detaching from thoughts, regularly practice separating awareness from thoughts.

TIP: Prolonged emotional distress is optional. If you are struggling with some powerful emotion like fear, anger, sadness, or grief, you may also still be able to schedule a no-cost, no-obligation one-on-one telephone session with me. If I'm still doing them, you may schedule the call at:

https://calendly.com/dennis-47/session

If you know any adults who are hurting emotionally, consider passing that tip along.

In addition to finding an effective strategy that works for you in terms of preventing the arising of powerful emotions in the first place, I'm able to help you with other tactics in addition to the Emotional Humility tactic, which can often quickly dissolve unwarranted, unwanted emotions after they arise. Sometimes such emotions can be troublesome for years or even decades. You may want to ask me about the Promoting Peacefulness tactic that can help eliminate such emotions in a lasting way – sometimes in very short order.

Bonus Chapter

[H]ere's "Chapter 1: How to Find the Purpose of Life" from my recent book <u>ARE YOU LIVING WITHOUT PURPOSE? The Simple Secret Nobody Tells You: How to Eliminate Anxiety</u>, which makes an excellent companion volume to <u>EMOTIONAL FACELIFT</u>. (For ease of reading here, I've eliminate its endnotes and the superscript numbers for them.)]

There's a secret to understanding the definitive answer to the question 'What is the purpose of life?'

As long as the question is considered in isolation, it lacks a definitive answer. Why?

Since there are a multiplicity of relevant, conflicting conceptual systems to which people attach, there are a multiplicity of different answers to that question that people actually accept. For example, a Christian might think that the correct answer is to serve [his or her conception of the Christian] God. A devotional Hindu might think that the correct answer is to engage in right ritual (orthopraxy, puja). A Daoist might think it's living in alignment with the values of naturalness, equanimity, spontaneity, and freedom. An artist might think it's creating beautiful works of art. A politician might think it's obtaining and holding political power. And so on and on.

The practical result is that there is serious confusion and disagreement about what we should be doing with our lives. It's understandable that many of us simply give up seeking a definitive answer, often by postponing indefinitely trying to answer the question.

It's good to be skeptical, questioning, about any important answer. However, it's not good simply to quit trying to understand the purpose of our lives. Such negativity merely adds to the usual heavy burden of anxiety.

Because answering the question is important, it's worth trying to answer it even though its solution is not ready-to-hand. What is it to live well? What is it to lead a meaningful life? What is it to fulfil the purpose of life? These questions are variations on a difficult theme.

It's both important to exclude related topics as well as not to overthink this topic. For example, a related topic would be the question about the purpose of the world. To answer the question about the purpose of life is not necessarily to answer all questions about purpose. An example of overthinking would be to distinguish a meaningful life from a purposeful life by thinking about the case of a death of an infant child. We might want to say that, even though that child's life had no purpose, it was nevertheless meaningful. Let's keep this discussion as simple as possible by identifying meaning and purpose. Perhaps we might agree that such a child simply never had the opportunity to live a purposeful life.

I argue that leading a meaningful or purposeful life is opening ordinary human life to the eternal. Since the reason we fail to do that is that we have become addicted to living in our thoughts, the way to lead a life of purpose is simply to drop thoughts, which automatically opens the temporal to the eternal. Like a nonhuman animal, an infant child is already open to the eternal because that child has not yet obscured the eternal by developing the capacity to live in the human world of our own making. If so, there's no difficulty about the purpose or meaning of that infant's life.

Even if the solution is that simple, it certainly doesn't *appear* to be that simple. It's not as if, for example, we could simply look somewhere to find the answer. Jesus made this point. For him, to live well was to live in "the kingdom of God" and he said, "You cannot tell by observation when the kingdom of God comes. There will be no saying, 'Look, here it is!' or 'there it is!'"

From the fact that there is no apparent solution it does not follow that there is no solution. It's true, though, that, as long as the question is considered abstractly, all there will ever be is a cacophony of answers based on different belief systems.

The reason for being optimistic about discovering a definitive answer is that these belief systems are all grounded on various different conceptions of being human. Might it be possible to agree about the nature of human being? Perhaps, but even that's unlikely.

However, what is possible is to agree about some feature of human being even if disagreement about other features remains. That, I suggest, is the way to a definitive answer to the question about our purpose.

So, *if* we could agree about a certain feature of human nature, we might agree that there is a definitive answer to the question of the purpose of human life.

There is such a feature of human nature. Linking that feature to the concept of purpose yields a definitive answer to the question of the purpose of human life.

Before considering that feature, what's not at issue here is our secondary or extrinsic purposes. Our topic is our <u>primary or intrinsic purpose</u>, which is the one we have simply by virtue of being human beings. <u>Secondary purposes</u> are roles or tasks that we adopt such as being a parent, being an author, being a carpenter, being a university student, and so on. There's nothing wrong with evaluating such purposes. They are important. Selecting those that match well with our abilities and skills is important for being happy. It's just that the purpose considered here is the one that we don't select because it's inherent in our nature.

Permit me an analogy to physics. I am not a physicist. Even if I were, physics is hardly a paradigm of knowledge; instead, it's a paradigm of rational belief. It's a system of conceptual understanding. The problem with any rational belief is that, even though it is rational, it may nevertheless be false. In the strict sense of 'knowledge,' which is the inconceivability of mistake, it is not knowledge. For example, if you were to ask a group of physicists why the expansion of the universe is accelerating, they may provide a rational guess or two, but they will ultimately just shake their heads. Is the speed of light really constant? Again, nobody really knows.

Still, using an analogy to physics may be helpful even though I must introduce another caveat: phenomenological or psychological time is not spacetime. Phenomenological or psychological time is simply time as we ordinarily experience it, as incessantly passing from the future via the present to the past. Spacetime is, supposedly, physical time, which is like a 4th dimension to ordinary three-dimensional space.

Here's the analogy: Einstein was the first to understand that, if the speed of light is constant, time itself is variable (as his familiar thought experiments suggest). Whether in fact the speed of light is constant is unimportant for the analogy: what matters is that it was part of the glory of Einstein's genius to connect the two ideas in that way.

Please consider the connection between our shared experiences of the passing of time with something constant. If something were not constant, how could we ever feel that time is passing? **What is constant cannot be time itself**. It is something "outside" time, something timeless, in other words, something eternal. Therefore, there is a feature of human being that is nontemporal.

If you are skeptical, as you should be, try thinking of it this way: if nothing were constant, we could never experience anything temporal, which is not constant. What is temporal is always in flux. Similarly, if everything in our visual field were always blue, because there'd be no contrast, we'd lack the concepts of other colors.

If so, any understanding of human nature that denies that we experience temporal flux or the flow of time would be *obviously inadequate*.

Therefore, minimally, a human being is a temporal being with a sense of the nontemporal. We have the concept of time, which means that we are able to separate that which is in time from that which is not in time.

Obviously, this is not a complete account of human nature. It doesn't have to be. It's merely a necessary condition of being human. There's not only something temporal about being human, but also there's something eternal about being human at least in the minimal sense that we have the concept of time. No time, no human being. No eternity, no human being.

Even if this point seems obvious, it becomes very important with respect to purpose. **To live well is to live a purposeful life**. What's that?

It's a life that is balanced between the temporal and the eternal. Why? Because living a life without balance would be ignoring a significant part of our human nature, which means that a significant part of our human nature would be automatically unfulfilled.

Words and concepts are never quite right – and those in the previous paragraph are a good example. The balance in question is not necessarily fifty-fifty like the two sides of a physical balance when the weights on each side are equal. My initial hope, though, is that the basic idea is clear: *if there are two necessary aspects (parts, sides, dimensions) of our nature (namely, the temporal and the eternal) and we ignore one, it would be impossible to live a purposeful [meaningful, fulfilled] life.*

In what follows, we'll consider the concrete implications what this means. The takeaway from this introductory chapter is this: **connecting the concept of purpose with the concept of time (temporality/eternity) is the secret key that yields a definitive answer to the question, 'What is the purpose of [human] life?'**

Our purpose is to fulfill both aspects of our nature; it is to be open to the eternal as well as the temporal.

Since everyone agrees that our lives are temporal, **in practice this means opening to the eternal**. To open to the eternal is to balance our lives between the temporal and the eternal. That's sufficient; in other words, it's unnecessary to specify how much openness to the eternal there must be.

Living well is being wise. Being wise is living a life in which the temporal and the eternal are open to each other. Being foolish, by way of contrast, is living a life that is closed to the eternal.

Sages have been saying this – although using different terminology and different conceptual systems – for thousands of years. It's not a new idea and it's not an idea original with me. If it were either, it would be shocking if the purpose of life were only discovered in the 21st century. It's an idea that goes back at least three thousand years.

Because, though, it's so easy to get so caught up in our everyday doings that it's possible to pretend that the eternal doesn't exist, it's still a critically important idea – at least for anyone interested in living well.

So let's next determine how you can tell if you are ripe for opening to that eternal aspect of your being or if you are closed to it. After all, except possibly for reinforcement, if you are already open to it, you don't need to read this book.